Studying the Presidency

Hugh Heclo

A REPORT TO THE FORD FOUNDATION

CONTENTS

Library of Congress Catalog Card Number 77-22035
ISBN 0-916584-07-0
August 1977

SUMMARY

This report has two main purposes: 1) to survey the present state of research on the Presidency and 2) to assess whether the Ford Foundation can make a significant contribution without duplicating work already in existence or underway.

The following discussion necessarily generalizes about—and thus does some injustice to—a large body of complex writing. Nevertheless, four basic conclusions seem clear:

1. *There is little likelihood that support will be needed for "new" topics in Presidential studies.* In terms of sheer mass of published material, the Presidency is probably already overwritten.

2. *Beneath the extensive veneer of Presidential literature, there are immense gaps and deficiencies.*
—There is a lack of basic empirical research. When original materials and documentation are used, they are often designed to prove some predetermined point.

5

—Too much attention is paid to Presidential power, personality, and crisis decisions; there is too little reliable, empirical analysis of how Presidential institutions and staff have actually functioned within and across different administrations.

—Little effort has been made to draw lessons of operational relevance for future administrations dealing with similar problems.

—The study of the modern Presidency has been too exclusively the domain of political scientists.

3. *Potentially, research opportunities to reduce these deficiencies are greater now than they ever were in the past.* However, research funds to take advantage of these opportunities are meager and poorly focused.

4. *Ford Foundation support could play an important and distinctive role* in encouraging substantive basic research on the Presidency.

PRESIDENTIAL STUDIES:
AN OVERVIEW

What appears to have been the first study of the Presidency as a social and political institution was written more than 150 years ago. On the eve of the Jacksonian Revolution, Augustus Woodward[1] produced a small tract foreshadowing most of the themes to be found in later work on the Presidency: Presidential selection and popular representation (as always, the electoral college needed to be reformed); problems of Presidential power inside the executive branch (the Cabinet was becoming too dominant); relations with Congress (they were strained because of administrative interference by the legislature); questions of Presidential staff (since important state documents were being lost, the President should have an official Secretary); executive secrecy, intelligence activities, and leaks; Presidential leadership in foreign policy (in Woodward's time, the problem was

1. Augustus B. Woodward, *The Presidency of the United States* (1825). Much earlier, when chief justice of the Michigan territory, Woodward had proposed a more collegial Presidency with one President and four elected councillors. *Considerations on the Executive Government of the United States* (1809).

foreigners meddling in our internal affairs); government management and reorganization (there needed to be a department to deal with domestic policies); Presidential advisory systems (rather than reliance on the emerging patronage system, the President should have more independent, expert advice from government officials); and managing the President's time (there should be less pomp and official entertainment but the President's people-to-people contact should be preserved by continuing the traditional right of any citizen to drop in on the President).

Attention to political and social developments outside Washington quickly eclipsed Woodward's effort to study the Presidency as an institution. During most of the 19th century, scholars gave only passing attention to the Presidency as a small part of the more general study of American government. Slowly at the turn of the century, however, and then more quickly after 1930, the Presidency emerged as a specialized area for research and interpretation.[2] As Presidents became a more prom-

2. Among the important landmarks are Edward Stanwood, *History of Presidential Elections* (1884) and *History of the Presidency from 1788-1897* (1898); H. C. Lockwood, *The Abolition of the Presidency* (1884), and Henry Jones Ford's prescient discussion of the Presidency in *The Rise and Growth of American Politics* (1898), chapters 15 and 22. Unlike today, the Presidents in those days were among the important contributors to this field of scholarship. See Grover Cleveland, *Presidential Problems* (1904); Woodrow Wilson, *Constitutional Government in the United States* (1908) (the section on the Presidency was reprinted in 1916 as *The President of the United States)*: the discussion of the President's inherent power in *Theodore Roosevelt: An Autobiography* (1913), and William Howard Taft's rejoinder in *Our Chief Magistrate and His Powers* (1916).

inent part of our national political life, academic studies followed apace and helped fulfill Alexander Hamilton's prophecy that the time would "come when every vital question of the state will be merged in the question, 'Who shall be the next President?'"[3] While calling the Presidency "understudied" and an "ignored waif," the authors of the most recent bibliography on the Presidency nevertheless list almost 3,000 entries published since the mid-1930s.[4] The Presidency industry has now grown to the point of producing innumerable books, conference reports, academic papers, and even a new quarterly journal.[5]

In fact, there appears to be no facet of the subject that has not been written about at one time or another in the last forty years—from the Presidency as an instrument of corporate capitalism (Bruce Miroff, *Pragmatic Illusions—The Presidential Politics of JFK,* 1976) to mathematical formulae for successfully dealing with Congress and the bureaucracy (Curtis Arthur Amlund, *New Perspectives on the Presidency,* 1969). Most of the existing research on the Presidency can be conveniently grouped into the same four categories that were at least implicit in Augustus Woodward's 1825 analysis: studies of 1) The man; 2) his linkages to the

3. Quoted in John C. Hamilton, *History,* vol. III, p. 335.

4. Fred I. Greenstein, Larry Berman, and Alvin S. Felzenberg, *Evolution of the Modern Presidency: A Bibliographical Survey* (American Enterprise Institute for Public Policy, 1977).

5. *Presidential Studies Quarterly,* published under the auspices of the Center for the Study of the Presidency in New York.

general population (what will be labeled here as Public Politics); 3) relations with other participants in the federal government (Washington Politics); and 4) the Presidency's in-house operations (Executive Politics). Finally there remains a large number of works—including the most widely known books on the Presidency—that seek to synthesize the previous categorical approaches and draw lessons about the office. This last category will be labeled here as Didactic Reviews.

The Man. The longest established and most luxuriant body of presidential literature tries to describe and/or analyze the man and his behavior. Not only biographies and collections of anecdotes but any number of other books can be put in this category insofar as they are primarily concerned with using events as a backdrop to ask the most popular and intriguing question about any given President: Who was this man?[6] Today's answers

6. Such books are numerous and often popular. A representative sample of recent studies would include, by administration: Bert Cochran, *Harry Truman and the Crisis Presidency* (1974); C. Phillips, *The Truman Presidency* (1966); A. L. Hamby, *Beyond the New Deal: Harry S. Truman and American Liberalism* (1973); Merle Miller, *Plain Speaking* (1974). M. Blumenson, *Eisenhower* (1972); H. S. Parmet, *Eisenhower of the American Crusades* (1972); A. Larson, *Eisenhower: The President Nobody Knew* (1968); Peter Lyon, *Eisenhower* (1974). L. J. Paper, *The Promise and the Performance: The Leadership of John F. Kennedy* (1975); E. Latham (ed.) *J. F. Kennedy and Presidential Power* (1972); Tom Wicker, *JFK and LBJ: The Influence of Personality Upon Politics* (1968). Eric F. Goldman, *The Tragedy of Lyndon Johnson* (1969); H. B. Johnson and R. Harwood, *Lyndon* (1973); Hugh Sidey, *A Very Personal Presidency* (1968). Roland Evans and Robert Novak, *Nixon in the White House* (1971); A. J. Hughes, *Richard M. Nixon* (1972); John Osborne, *The Last Nixon Watch* (1975); G. Allen, *Richard Nixon, The Man Behind the Mask* (1971).

range from the fairly superficial gossip about Presidents' private lives to attempts at in-depth psychological analysis.[7]

Between these two extremes there have developed suggestive middle-range studies of Presidential behavior. Here the effort is not so much to unearth the basic psychological motives of a man who happens to be President as to understand the interplay of style and character that produces a President's standard operating procedures. The basic orienting principle of this approach has been expressed in David Barber's dictum that "The Presidency exists solely in the minds of men."[8]

What, apart from satisfying our curiosity about particular individuals, is to be gained by examining the psychology of Presidents? More than might at first appear. Traditional checklists of required Presidential qualities remain as vague and homiletic as ever;[9] by most accounts, Presidents should have all the good qualities of the "great" and "strong" Presidents of the past and none of their bad qualities. Recently, however, middle-range studies of Presidential character have managed to elicit

7. Clay Blair, Jr., *The Search for John F. Kennedy* (1976); Doris Kearns, *Lyndon Johnson and the American Dream* (1976); Alexander L. George and Juliette L. George, *Woodrow Wilson and Colonel House* (1956); Bruce Mazlish, *In Search of Nixon* (1972);David Abrahamsen, *Nixon vs. Nixon* (1977).

8. James David Barber, *The Presidential Character* (1971), p. 450.

9. Malcolm Parsons, "The Presidential Rating Game," in Charles W. Dunn, *The Future of the American Presidency* (1975); Joseph E. Kallenbach, *The American Chief Executive* (1966), pp. 257-69; Morton Borden, *America's Eleven Greatest Presidents* (1971).

generalizations that seem more reliable. Some critics have raised questions about this kind of analysis and its predictive merit,[10] but the fact remains that of all the early writings about the new Nixon administration,[11] only Barber's account managed to predict the outlines of Nixon's personal catastrophe in the White House. Given this initial success and the surrounding publicity, studies in Presidential character and psychology seem likely to continue growing in the years ahead.

Public Politics. Relations between the Presidency and the public at large are covered by four major types of studies: 1) selection and election of Presidents, 2) popularity and public images of Presidents, 3) Presidential communications with the public through the media, and 4) linkages between the President and public through political parties.

In the first category are a large number of books and articles concerned with choosing Presidents. A recent trend has been to supplement traditional election studies with more detailed attention to the pre-election selection process that produces the parties' candidates.[12] A major,

10. Alexander L. George, "Assessing Presidential Character," *World Politics* (1974).

11. Such studies generally tried to assess the White House policy process without considering the important personal factors affecting this process. See, for example, R. Gordon Hoxie (ed.), *The White House: Organization and Operations* (1971); John H. Kessel, *The Domestic Presidency* (1975).

12. James W. Davis, *Springboard to the White House: Presidential Primaries* (1967); Melvyn H. Bloom, *Public Relations and Presidential Cam-*

and still unresolved, question is whether revisions in the campaign laws, growth in the number of primaries, decline in party voting, and reforms in party organization will, individually or in combination, produce fundamental changes in the dynamics of Presidential selection.[13]

The second category of studies in the President's public politics concerns popularity and the public's image of the President. How is the Presidency perceived?[14] How does a President's popularity wax and wane, and what difference does variation in popularity make in Presidential policy? Since the Second World War, enough polling evidence has accumulated to provide a number of useful generalizations and distinctions.[15] Public opinion studies suggest, for example, that:

---

paigns (1973); Michael Novak, *Choosing Our King* (1974); William R. Keech and Donald R. Matthews, *The Party's Choice* (1976); Arthur Hadley, *The Invisible Primary* (1976).

13. Nelson Polsby and Aaron Wildavsky, *Presidential Elections* (1976 edition); James R. Beniger, "Polls and Primaries," *Public Opinion Quarterly* (1976); J. W. Ceaser, "The Theory and Development of Presidential Selection" (in progress), University of Virginia. *N.B.:* Here and throughout, the citation of an institution of higher learning indicates that the work is an unpublished manuscript.

14. Even the perceptions of children in this respect have received considerable attention. See, for example, Fred. I. Greenstein, *Children and Politics* (1965); David Easton and Jack Dennis, *Children in the Political System* (1969); F. C. Arterton, "The Impact of Watergate on Childrens' Attitudes Toward Political Authority," *Political Science Quarterly* (June 1974).

15. Milton Rosenberg, Sidney Verba, and Philip Converse, *Vietnam and the Silent Majority* (1971); Stuart G. Brown, *The American Presidency* (1966); John E. Mueller, *War, Presidents and Public Opinion* (1973); James A. Stimson, "Public Support for American Presidents," *Public Opinion Quarterly* (1976).

—Presidents can retain personal popularity even while their particular policies are being rejected;

—Presidential actions can sometimes quickly convert unpopular policies to popular ones;

—Not all kinds of Presidential popularity are equally convertible into policy support;

—Every contemporary President can expect his popularity rating to follow the path of a U-shaped curve, but no President is likely to leave office with as high a popular rating as the one with which he arrived.

Since polling and other data gauging public opinion are constantly accumulating and readily accessible to political scientists, Presidential popularity is likely to continue as a well-cultivated subfield in the study of the Presidency. At a more general level, questions have been raised about basic social changes that may be transforming the traditional capacities of the Presidency to deal with public opinion.[16] However, in this area the major line of advance appears to lie in broader studies of political sociology and political economy[17] rather than in Presidential research per se.

A third aspect of the Presidency's public politics has attracted writers concerned with the media. Numerous studies have documented the changing character and techniques of Presidential communications with the

16. George E. Reedy, *The Presidency in Flux* (1973).

17. Norman Nie and Sidney Verba, *The Changing American Voter* (1975); Morris Janowitz, *Social Control of the Welfare State* (1976).

general public.[18] Likewise, the rhetoric of Presidential persuasion has produced a steady flow of writing, particularly from academics in schools of speech and journalism.[19] Only in recent years has more attention been paid to the content of Presidential and executive branch communication with the public. The most fertile fields for such research appear to be in the areas of misinformation and unnecessary secrecy[20] — an unfortunate reflection on recent history.

The final area of a President's public politics — his position as party leader — is normally an obligatory topic in most textbooks on the Presidency, but few works have attempted to describe Presidential party operations in any detail.[21] Scholars have usually followed the lead pro-

18. Elmer E. Cornwell, Jr., *Presidential Leadership of Public Opinion* (1965); James Keogh, *President Nixon and the Press* (1972); James F. Pollard, *The Presidents and the Press* (1964); Robert E. Gilbert, *Television and Presidential Politics* (1972); Meyer Stein, *When Presidents Meet the Press* (1969).

19. Harry Sharp, Jr., "The Kennedy News Conference," Purdue University (1967); Anne Elizabeth Kyes, "President Kennedy's Press Conferences as 'Shapers' of the News," University of Iowa (1968); Jerome B. Polisky, "The Kennedy-Nixon Debates: A Study in Political Persuasion," University of Wisconsin (1965); Walter L. Schneider, "Spoken Rhetoric and Its Application to the United States Presidency," University of California, Berkeley (1968); Jerrold J. Merchant, "Kennedy-Khrushchev Strategies of Persuasion During the Cuban Missile Crisis," University of Southern California (1971).

20. David Wise, *The Politics of Lying* (1973); William Porter, *Assault on the Media* (1975); Edward Knappman, *Government and the Media in Conflict* (1974); John Herbers, *No Thank You, Mr. President* (1976); Marvin Barrett (ed.), *Moments of Truth?* (1975).

21. Cornelius P. Cotter and Bernard C. Hennessy, *Politics Without Power: The National Party Committees* (1964); Herbert S. Parmet, *The Democrats: The Years After FDR* (1976); Howard Bass, "Structural and Organiza-

vided by studies of voting habits. Since these studies have documented a progressive decline in party voting, writers on the Presidency have found it more rewarding and realistic to concentrate on Presidents' linkages to the public through the media and public relations techniques rather than through their party activities. The result is that while there is widespread acceptance of the view that the President's party role has generally atrophied, there is extraordinarily little empirical information on how Presidents are conducting (or avoiding) party business and how this situation may have been developing over the years.

Washington Politics. Under this category can be grouped all those works that put primary emphasis on the relations between President and other major institutions in the Washington community.

By far the largest portion of this literature is devoted to interactions between the Presidency and Congress. The most broad-gauged books on this topic focus on the question of relative power: Is the President or Congress gaining the upper hand?[22] For a considerable period the

---

tional Changes in the President's Role as Party Leader, 1945-1972," Vanderbilt University (in progress); R. M. Goldman, "Titular Leadership of Presidential Parties," in Aaron Wildavsky (ed.), *The Presidency* (1969).

22. Ronald Moe (ed.), *Congress and the President* (1971); Louis Fisher, *The President and Congress* (1972); Nelson W. Polsby, *Congress and the Presidency* (1976 edition); James L. Sundquist, *The Decline and Resurgence of Congress* (in progress); Harvey C. Mansfield (ed.), *Congress Against the President* (1975); John Lehmen, *The Executive, Congress and Foreign Policy* (1976).

verdicts ran in the President's favor, but since the collapse of the Nixon administration, there has been considerable shift of opinion in Congress's favor.

Below this level of general interpretation, research emphasis has been on case studies of particular bills and programs.[23] In fact this programmatic approach has been utilized in the only attempt in recent years to organize resources in a Presidential library by functional category. Materials concerning education and civil rights legislation were organized separately at the Johnson library, but before the effort could extend to other areas it was aborted by the former President's death. Nevertheless, at graduate schools across the country there is a ceaseless, disorganized, and non-cummulative flow of dissertations studying particular cases of Presidential/Congressional interaction. There are far fewer accounts of the Presidency's own organization and the evolution of its methods for dealing with Congress, e.g., the postwar development of the White House Congressional Liaison Office, legislative clearance operations, and so on.[24]

During most of the postwar "behavioral movement" in political science, Presidential relations with the legal

23. Two of the most ambitious and well-rounded such studies are Raymond Bauer et al., *American Business and Public Policy* (1963); and a ten-year project in progress at the School of Education, University of Michigan, to study postwar education policy. See too, Graeme W. Starr, "The Politics of the U.S. Trade Expansion Program, 1962-1967," West Virginia University (1969); Roy E. Young, "Presidential Leadership and Civil Rights Legislation, 1963-1964, University of Texas, Austin (1969); David W. Folts, "The Role of the President and Congress in the Formulation of United States Eco-

system and courts were downplayed as unduly formalistic. However, since the Vietnam War and Watergate, the public law approach has undergone a strong revival in Presidential studies. Gaps obviously remain (Willard Humbert's *The Pardoning Power of the President,* 1941, is still the standard work on the subject being used by the Justice Department), but the last ten years have seen important work on Presidential war powers, executive privilege, budgeting, and impeachment, among other subjects.[25] There has not yet appeared a comprehensive public law text on the Presidency that would bring Corwin or Schubert up to date,[26] but given the high level of research activity in a number of law schools, this situation is likely to change in the near future. Research into primary sources on the early years of the Presidency

nomic Policy Towards the Soviet Union, 1947-1968," University of Notre Dame (1971); John M. Logsdon, III, *The Decision to Go to the Moon: Project Apollo and the National Interest* (1970).

24. Abraham Holtzman, *Legislative Liaison* (1970); Edward de Grazia, *Congressional Liaison* (1965); Robert S. Gilmour, "Central Legislative Clearance, A Revised Perspective," *Public Administration Review* (1971); Stephen Wayne, "The Legislative Presidency," George Washington University (in progress).

25. Francis D. Wormuth, *The Vietnam War: The President Versus the Constitution* (1968); Louis Henkin, *Foreign Affairs and the Constitution* (1972); Leon Friedman and Burt Neuborne, *Unquestioning Obedience to the President: The ACLU Case* (1972); Raoul Berger, *Impeachment* (1973) and *Executive Privilege* (1974); Adam Carlyle Breckenridge, *The Executive Privilege* (1974); Louis Fisher, *Presidential Spending Power* (1975); William Van Alstyne, "A Political and Constitutional Review of *United States* v. *Nixon,"* *UCLA Law Review* (1974); Robert Scigliano, *The Supreme Court and the Presidency* (1971).

26. Glendon Schubert, *The Presidency in the Courts* (1957); Edward S. Corwin, *The President: Office and Powers* (1957 edition).

18

has already uncovered important new evidence that will require scholars to reconsider a good deal of the conventional wisdom about formal Presidential powers.[27]

While Presidential/Congressional tensions have been a staple research subject and the new jurisprudence approach to the Presidency has grown, study of interactions between the Presidency and the rest of the executive branch has been a major nongrowth area. A few studies have been written on the Cabinet, or, more broadly, on the use Presidents can and should make of agency and department heads. During every recent administration such studies have argued that the President should make better use of his Cabinet, but for almost no administration is there good empirical evidence as to why these injunctions have usually not been carried out.[28]

Below the more glamorous Cabinet level, there is again a large assortment of case studies concerning particular programs in the bureaucracy.[29] Only rarely, however, has research on the Presidency systematically delved into interactions between the Presidency and operational reality in the bureaucracy. A major excep-

27. Abraham D. Sofaer, *War, Foreign Affairs, and Constitutional Powers* (1976).

28. Richard F. Fenno, Jr., *The President's Cabinet* (1959); Henry F. Graff, *The Tuesday Cabinet* (1970); Bradley H. Patterson, Jr., *The President's Cabinet: Issues and Questions* (1976).

29. The number of books, articles, and dissertations of this nature is clearly immense. A personal survey by the author suggested that almost one-half of the research projects underway and using the resources of the Kennedy and Johnson libraries could be placed in this category.

tion to this generalization is in the area of defense and foreign policy, where "bureaucratic politics" has been recently revived as an interpretive framework.[30] But the fact remains that we know more about Presidents' social habits than about the underlying causes of the widely publicized charges of bureaucratic unresponsiveness to Presidential leadership, particularly in domestic policy issues. There is little systematic evidence on how the bureaucracy problem has manifested itself in different administrations, the various means used in the White House for coping with it, and the efficacy of different strategies.

Executive Politics. This heading embraces studies that are concerned less with Presidential relations with "outsiders"—Congress, parties, the bureaucracy, general public, and so on—and more with interactions between and among those people in the White House Office or Executive Office of the President who act in the President's name. Books and articles on Presidential advisers deal with everything from the personal attributes of the people in daily contact with the President[31]

30. I. M. Destler, *Presidents, Bureaucrats, and Foreign Policy* (1972); Morton H. Halperin, *Bureaucratic Politics and Foreign Policy* (1974); Robert T. Sullivan, "The Role of the Presidency in Shaping Lower Level Policy-Making Processes," *Polity* (1970); David S. Brown, "The President and the Bureaus," *Public Administration Review* (1966).

31. Patrick Anderson, *The President's Men* (1968); Louis W. Koenig, *The Invisible Presidency* (1960); Charles Roberts, *LBJ's Inner Circle* (1965); Dan Rather and Gary Paul Gates, *The Palace Guard* (1974); Joseph Kraft, *Profiles in Power* (1966).

to the impersonal advisory commissions whose reports Presidents often file and forget.[32]

Apparently spurred by events of recent years, writers have begun paying considerably more attention to Presidential staff in the White House Office.[33] Unlike earlier works, these recent efforts are less concerned with particular personalities and more with general problems of internal organization. Typical questions posed are: What are the alternatives for organizing the President's staff? What are the likely consequences of different models? So far at least, there are few widely accepted answers to these general questions. More detailed studies of the White House policy process have usually been dominated by concerns with the Vietnam War.[34] Only a few works, such as those by Neustadt and Hess, have managed to convey a sense of the everyday dynamics by which various institutional and personal advisers interact to affect the substance of information coming to and

---

32. Thomas R. Wolanin, *Presidential Advisory Commissions* (1975); Thomas E. Cronin and Sanford D. Greenburg, *The Presidential Advisory System* (1969); George Grassmuck, "White House Conferences," University of Wisconsin (in progress); Frank Popper, *The President's Commissions* (1970); J. T. Sulzner, "The Policy Process and the Uses of National Government Study Commissions," *Western Politics Quarterly* (1971).

33. Richard Tanner Johnson, *Managing the White House* (1974); Michael B. Grossman and Martha Kumar, "White House Staff Officials," Towson State University (in progress); Richard Rose, "The President: 'A Chief but not an Executive'," Strathclyde University (in progress); Lewis A. Dexter, "Court Politics: Presidential Staff Relations as a Special Case," paper to the 1976 convention, American Political Science Association.

34. Irving L. Janis, *Victims of Groupthink* (1972); David Halberstam, *The Best and the Brightest* (1972); John C. Donovan, *The Cold Warriors* (1974).

the quality of decisions flowing out of the Presidency.[35] There are, of course, a large number of retrospective accounts by White House staff of the internal dynamics of the particular Presidency with which they happened to be personally involved.[36] Frequently, subsequent academic writing has been highly derivative of these secondary sources, often accepting their unsubstantiated generalizations at face value.

By far the largest amount of empirical research on executive politics has focused on specific cases of Presidential decision-making during national security crises. The results range from a huge number of descriptive monographs,[37] to a lesser number of more theoretical

35. Richard E. Neustadt, *Presidential Power* (1976 edition); Stephen Hess, *Organizing the Presidency* (1976).

36. Among the more widely read are Roger Hilsman, *To Move a Nation* (1967); Dean Acheson, *Present at the Creation* (1969); William Safire, *Before the Fall* (1975); Theodore Sorensen, *Kennedy* (1965); Lawrence O'Brien, *No Final Victories* (1974); Joseph A. Califano, Jr., *A Presidential Nation* (1975); Richard Nathan, *The Plot that Failed* (1975).

37. Writings on the Cuban missile crisis can be taken as a prominent example of this genre. See Robert E. Cecile, "Crisis Decision-Making in the Eisenhower and Kennedy Administrations," University of Oklahoma (1965); Walter W. Layson, "The Political and Strategic Aspects of the 1962 Cuban Crisis," University of Virginia (1969); Allan M. Parrent, "The Responsible Use of Power: The Cuban Missile Crisis in Christian Perspective," Duke University (1969); Raymond A. Rimkus, "The Cuban Missile Crisis: A Decision-Making Analysis of The Quarantine Policy with Special Emphasis Upon the Implication for Decision-Making Theory," University of Oklahoma (1971); Bernard H. Ross, "American Government in Crisis: An Analysis of the Executive Branch of Government During the Cuban Missile Crisis," New York University (1971); William G. Skillern, "An Analysis of the Decision-Making Process in the Cuban Missile Crisis," University of Idaho (1971). For a more general study with an extensive bibliography, see Alexander George, *The Limits of Coercive Diplomacy* (1971).

works that try to use these events to generate broader models of the policy process.[38] Unfortunately, crisis studies as a means of understanding the Presidency have shortcomings. They ignore the fact that a great deal of the internal operations in the Presidency are aimed at something other than producing decisions. Presumably White House staffs also help Presidents avoid, temporize about, reconsider, and elaborate on decisions. Moreover, decisions, when they are made, only rarely have the characteristics of those involving a national crisis—which is to say that the President is not usually operating as an hour-by-hour executive officer at the top of a clear (if not always reliable) chain of command.

Writers on the Presidency have naturally been attracted to the high drama of court politics and crisis decision-making in the White House. There has been far less interest in studying the everyday work flow and operations of Presidential institutions and staff. This is particularly true for the enduring units in the Executive Office of the President. Obviously, research has been done on the Office of Management and Budget,[39] Coun-

38. Graham T. Allison, *The Essence of Decision* (1971); Abram Chayes, *The Cuban Missile Crisis* (1974); Thomas Halper, *Foreign Policy Crises: Appearance and Reality in Decision-Making* (1970); Graham Allison and Peter Szanton, *Remaking Foreign Policy* (1976); I. M. Destler, "National Security Advice to Presidents," *World Politics* (1977).

39. Gary Bombardier, "The Managerial Function of OMB," *Public Policy* (1975); Allen Schick, "The Bureau of the Budget that Was," *Law and Contemporary Problems* (1970); Hugh Heclo, "OMB and the Presidency," *The Public Interest* (1975); Aaron Wildavsky, *The Politics of the Budgetary Pro-*

23

cil of Economic Advisers,[40] and especially the National Security Council.[41] The point, however, is that considering the important responsibilities lodged in these staffs, there is remarkably little in-depth research on the operations, development, and performance records of these and other parts the Executive Office of the President. By and large the promising beginnings that were made some two decades ago in the study of the President's Executive Office have not been seriously pursued.[42]

cess (1964). In the last twenty-five years there has been no book devoted to analyzing the central organization and operation of the budget process within the Executive Office of the President.

40. Edward S. Flash, *Economic Advice and Presidential Leadership* (1965); Hugh Norton, *The Role of the Economist in Government* (1969) and *The Council of Economic Advisers: Three Periods of Influence* (1973); David Naveh, "The Council of Economic Advisers," University of Connecticut (in progress).

41. Keith Clark and Lawrence Legere (eds.), *The President and the Management of National Security* (1969); Arthur Cox, *The Myths of National Security* (1975); Clark Murdock, *Defense Policy Formation* (1974); Warren Hassler, *The President as Commander-in-Chief* (1971); Richard Johnson, "The National Security Council," *Orbis* (1969); C. L. Figliola, "Considerations of National Security Administration," *Public Administration Review* (1974).

42. John Steelman and H.D. Kraeger, "The Executive Office as Administrative Coordinator," *Law and Contemporary Problems* (1956); Clinton Rossiter, "The Constitutional Significance of the Executive Office of the President," *American Political Science Review* (1949); Lester Seligman, "Presidential Leadership, the Inner Circle and Institutionalization," *Journal of Politics* (1956); Richard E. Neustadt, "Presidency and Legislation, the Growth of Central Clearance," *American Political Science Review* (1954); Edward Hobbs, *Behind the President: A Study of Executive Office Agencies* (1954). A recent exception to this neglect, is Larry Berman's doctoral dissertation at Princeton University, "The Evolution of a Presidential Staff Agency: Variations In How the Bureau of the Budget-OMB Has Responded to Presidential Needs" (1977).

24

Didactic Reviews. Once one has categorized the Presidential studies that fall more or less readily into the preceding four areas, there obviously still remains a large body of literature to be accounted for. In fact, these remaining works constitute what are usually regarded as the core of Presidential scholarship. Their basic feature is that they knit together the previous categories—the man, his public politics, Washington politics, and executive politics—into general accounts that seek to instruct the reader. Almost invariably, the subject of that instruction is Presidential power.

The major theme to be found in didactic literature on the Presidency is that the President's power is that of persuasion rather than command. His strength does not lie in his purely administrative abilities but in the moral leadership and vision by which he influences others to do what they should be doing anyway. This basic didactic theme can be traced at least as far back as Woodrow Wilson, into the work of Laski, Brownlow, Neustadt, Egger, among many others, and on into the most recent "reappraisals" of the Presidency.

Apart from the several works (such as Neustadt's *Presidential Power)* that try to suggest strategic lessons for Presidential use, the dominant analytic aim in the synthesizing books is to render judgments on Presidential power. How has this power grown? Has it grown too much or not enough? What should be done about it? These are the questions that provide the focus for what is literally a host of individual books and articles, edited volumes, and conference reports by Presidential experts.[43] A few of these interpretations have become the dominant classics of a particular period—the works of Corwin, Koenig, Finer, Burns, Rossiter, Schlesinger, for example. Most, however, for one reason or another, have tended to become deadweight on bookshelves.

Interpretations of Presidential power are obviously important, and certainly the recent resurgence of interest in the legal powers of Presidents is overdue. Not too many years ago, Presidents Howard Taft and Theodore Roosevelt debated the question of Presidential power in terms of whether the President required specific legislative or Constitutional directives in order to act (Taft), or whether the President was free to act unless specifically forbidden to do so by such directives (Roosevelt). By 1973, the issue had evolved to the point where a former top government official could seriously advance the proposition that "there are times when the President

43. Here it is possible to list only a few of the more recent additions. Among the books are Ernest S. Griffith, *The American Presidency: The Dilemmas of Shared Power and Divided Government* (1976); Emmet John Hughes, *The Living Presidency* (1973); Erwin C. Hargrove, *The Power of the Modern Presidency* (1974); Charles Hardin, *Presidential Power and Accountability* (1974); Thomas E. Cronin, *The State of the Presidency* (1975); Grant McConnell, *The Modern Presidency* (1976 ed.). Among the many edited volumes are Charles Roberts (ed.), *Has the President Too Much Power* (1974); Aaron Wildavsky (ed.), *The Presidency* (1969), and *Perspectives on the Presidency* (1975); Charles Dunn (ed.), *The Future of the American Presidency* (1975); Nelson W. Polsky (ed.), *The Modern Presidency* (1973); Norman C. Thomas (ed.), *The Presidency in Contemporary Context* (1975); Philip Dolce and Jeorge Skau (eds.), *Power and the Presidency* (1976); William Lammers (ed.), *Presidential Politics* (1976); Rexford Tugwell and Thomas Cronin (eds.), *The Presidency Reappraised* (1974).

of the United States would be right in not obeying a decision of the Supreme Court."[44]

The literature of Presidential power has generally followed cycles of reacting positively or negatively to experiences with the most recent man in the White House. Writing after the Franklin D. Roosevelt years, some experts put primary emphasis on worrying about the growth of the President's independent power (Edward S. Corwin, *The President: Office and Powers,* 1948 edition) while others, recalling the growing challenge of totalitarianism in the 1930s, saw the same phenomenon as benign proof that democracy could act swiftly and vigorously in an emergency. (Louis Brownlow, *The President and the Presidency,* 1949). A decade later Presidential scholars reacted to the Eisenhower administration's passivity and institutionalized staff system and felt either reassured (Corwin, *The President: Office and Powers,* 1957 edition), or worried (Herman Finer, *The Presidency: Crisis and Regeneration,* 1960; Rexford Tugwell, *The Enlargement of the Presidency,* 1960), but mainly, it seems, impatient for a return to Presidential activism (Clinton Rossiter, *The American Presidency,* 1960; Francis H. Heller, *The Presidency: A Modern Perspective,* 1960).

Since 1960 the cycle has obviously taken another turn. Midway through the Johnson Administration, one writer reflected that Presidents had become so success-

44. John Connally, quoted in Theodore Sorensen, *Watchmen in the Night* (1973), p. 48.

ful in creating a consensus on freedom and equality that the Presidency might be overpowering other political institutions and running out of legitimate Presidential goals (James MacGregor Burns, *Presidential Government,* 1966). The Vietnam War and Nixon Administration led to more immediate worries. These worries concerned the excesses of Presidential-cum-bureaucratic power (Dorothy Buckton James, *The Contemporary Presidency,* 1969) and, above all, the potential for and reality of abuse of power. Sometimes these varying cyclical emphases may be traced in different books by the same author, sometimes in different editions of the same book, and sometimes even in different chapters of books caught in midpassage by unusual events—by the Watergate crisis, for example.

None of this is meant to suggest that the grand synthesizers of the Presidency are necessarily inconsistent or biasing their accounts to support personal preferences for the policies or person of a particular President. The point is only that Presidential scholars, like everyone else, see and are inclined to interpret the Presidency in the light of immediate experience. The lessons emphasized in the literature of Presidential didactics change with the latest judgments about the merits and demerits of what "he" is doing to "us." This may be a good recipe for writing trenchant interpretations of current events, but it does not provide in-depth empirical information about what is actually happening in the Presidency as an institution.

In the current atmosphere there is little need to encourage further studies about controlling the Presidency and preventing abuses of power. At this point in the cycle, the major propositions being advanced in Presidential didactics appear to be roughly as follows: 1) Presidents have grown more powerful vis-a-vis the traditionally competing political forces (viz., Congress, Cabinet officers, other party leaders, and so on); 2) but the use of Presidential power has also become more constrained by rising public expectations and the complexity of problems Presidents face; and 3) therefore, Presidential power should not be weakened; but 4) it should be made more accountable to Congress, the legal system, and the public at large. When the cycle swings again and there is less attention to abuses and more to incapacities of a President, there will likewise be little need to encourage Presidential scholars to write about the need to strengthen the President's hand to meet urgent national needs (e.g., in economic policy, energy, foreign affairs, and so on).

CURRENT RESEARCH:
DEFICIENCIES AND CORRECTIVES

Recently, the search committee of a major midwestern university tried to fill an important professorial chair in the Presidency. After more than a year of looking for a "good, bright guy who is doing interesting things," the committee concluded that almost no one was. Given some exaggeration, this seems a reasonable verdict of much of what is currently going on in the field of Presidential studies. Political observers have written excellent interpretations of the Presidency. Important questions about Presidential power have been raised. But considering the amount of such writing in relation to the base of original empirical research behind it, the field is as shallow as it is luxuriant. To a great extent, presidential studies have coasted on the reputations of a few rightfully respected classics on the Presidency and on secondary literature and anecdotes produced by former participants. We still have remarkably little substantiated information on how the modern office of the President actually works. There are at least three major reasons for rendering such a harsh judgment on what are, after all, a large number of well-intentioned publications.

1. A Lack of Basic Research in Primary Materials. Presidential studies have been largely the domain of political scientists; yet the basis of much Presidential interpretation lies in historical materials. Unlike Congressional scholars, researchers on the Presidency cannot operate on site and personally watch ongoing operations within the West Wing of the White House. Instead, Presidential scholarship must normally depend on careful political and historical research in the written records and critical analysis of the accounts of those who have worked there. As research interests range beyond the White House compound (e.g., operations in Executive Office units or government bureaus), more direct observation can be counted on to supplement historical sources.

The fact is that only rarely in recent years has there been the kind of in-depth historical-cum-political science research that would provide a reliable factual basis for judging everyday operations in the Presidency and/or executive branch. It is noteworthy, for example, that Leonard White's final volume, covering the years 1869- 1901, was the last major administrative history of how government business has been conducted.[1] For our own postwar period, many summary judgments on the Presidency have been presented with only cursory evidential

1. Leonard D. White, *The Republican Era* (1958). Under the direction of Emmette Redford, attempts are being made to launch an administrative history of the Johnson years at the University of Texas in Austin, and, in May 1977, a conference on an administrative history of the Truman years was held in Kansas City, Missouri, under the auspices of the Truman Library Institute.

backing. The Presidential office is said to have become more institutionalized with a large bureaucracy of its own, and yet it is also said to have become more personalized with each succeeding President. Massive attention is devoted to the special characteristics of particular Presidents but "something" about the office seems to be forcing all Presidents into similar willful behavior patterns. The nature of that something remains a mystery. At a recent conference of presidential experts, some participants were "terrified" at the potential implications of Nixon's efforts to institute a "Departmental Responsiveness Program" for political purposes and to use White House staff to cudgel department heads; other participants were untroubled and had little difficulty citing analogies from previous administrations.[2] In 1949, Louis Brownlow opposed the then current proposals to establish a Cabinet secretariat, but argued that as "manager-in-chief" the President would have to find a systematic way of bringing about teamwork among department heads and Executive Office staff on problems that cut across agency jurisdictions.[3] Similarly, since the end of the Johnson Presidency and on into the Nixon and Carter administrations, the conventional wisdom has been that the President needs new institutional mechanisms to cope with interdepartmental problems. But in terms of

2. "Highlights of a Conference on the Institutional Presidency," held at Airlie House, Warrenton, Virginia, April 11-13, 1974, pp. 7 and 21 of transcript.

3. Louis Brownlow, *The President and The Presidency* (1949), pp. 131-132.

32

any precise understanding of what has changed in the requirements for Presidential management, why, and what can be done about it, reformers have little more empirical information and substantial research to draw upon today than Brownlow had 30 years ago.[4]

An example may help clarify what is meant by a lack of basic research. One of the most widespread observations on the Presidency in recent years has concerned its growing size: the Presidency has become not simply larger but "swollen," "bloated," "bureaucratized," and so on. If an empirical indicator is used to support these criticisms, it is invariably the growth in the number of Presidential staff. Frequently such figures are borrowed second or third hand from established Presidential scholars, and, at times, White House Office staff is misleadingly lumped in with the number of staff in the Executive Office of the President. Such figures are misleading because changes in the latter frequently have little to do with Presidential aggrandizement and a great deal to do with outside interests that wish to highlight a particular issue (e.g., economic opportunity, consumer affairs, drug en-

4. There are, of course, some exceptions. Research in hitherto unstudied archival material has helped clarify some of the story for earlier periods, e.g., Barry Karl, *Executive Reorganization and Reform in the New Deal* (1963). Another example is the work of Peri Arnold at Notre Dame: "Reorganization and Politics," *Public Administration Review* (1974); and "Executive Reorganization and Administrative Theory: The Origin of the Managerial Presidency," paper to the 1976 American Political Science Convention (September 2-5, 1976). An example of interesting research underway for the current period is Roger Porter's Ph.D. dissertation at Harvard on Presidential coordination of economic policy-making.

forcement) by using a letterhead from the Executive Office of the President.

However, serious writers on the Presidency are aware of this situation and typically cite growth only in the White House Office. The data in common currency are startling—from a staff of 45 in FDR's White House to more than 600 in Nixon's Presidency. But these data depend, in turn, on various efforts to count White House staff using the yearly appropriation requests submitted to Congress.[5] There has been little effort to qualify the numbers by considering the problem of employees appointed to an agency and detailed back to the White House Office.[6]

An alternative method of counting would be to use primary materials and add the numbers of detailed employees into the total. This might then suggest that the swelling of the Presidency has been far less than usually asserted (see Table). Instead of a sixteenfold increase since FDR, the growth in this total number of White House staff would be seen to be slightly over three times—a change that does not seem too remarkable in terms of growth in other government agencies and in

5. House Committee on Post Office and Civil Service, *A Report of the Executive Office of the President,* April 24, 1972; Howard E. McCurdy, "The Physical Manifestations of an Expanded Presidency," paper at 1974 American Political Science Convention, Chicago, 1974.

6. The House committee report assumes that the number of detailees in 1955 and 1965 were the same as in 1970. McCurdy suggests that the numbers in any given year should be increased by 20 per cent to take account of detailees to the White House.

executive responsibilities since the pre-World War II years. The figures might also suggest why both President Truman in 1947 and President Nixon in 1971 aroused public criticism over growth in their White House staffs —they published a relatively comprehensive count.

The rejoinder is likely to be that mere numbers do not tell the real story, and, of course, that is true. In FDR's White House, staff positions may have represented lower level people who were doing different things (particularly not interposing themselves between the President and agency heads) than were members of the larger, high level staff in Nixon's White House. The point is that more careful quantitative work on the Presidency may help, but it cannot substitute for in-depth, systematic research on what people connected with the Presidency have actually done, and on how well their arrangements have managed to deal with the substantive problems of government. Simply on the question of detailed employees, it is important to know how far this process has been a means by which staff with operational experience in the departments are actually brought within the ambit of White House policy-making, and how far it has been merely a *pro forma* reassignment of slots to conceal the actual number of full-time White House staff.

2. *Operational Irrelevance.* It is said that a stack of paper two feet high comes across the President's desk each day for signature. There are, it is probably safe to say, no Presidential scholars who could offer a reasoned estimate

White House Office Staff

Fiscal Year	Full-Time Employees		Published Total	Detailed Employees*	Actual Total
	Regular	Special Projects			
1934	45	—	45	120	165
1935	45	—	45	127	172
1936	45	—	45	115	160
1937	45	—	45	112	157
1938	45	—	45	119	164
1939	45	—	45	112	157
1940	63	—	63	114	177
1941	62	—	62	117	179
1942	47	—	47	137	184
1943	46	—	46	148	194
1944	47	—	47	145	192
1945	48	—	48	167	215
1946	51	—	51	162	213
1947	190	—	190	27	217
1948	245	—	245	23	268
1949	220	—	220	26	246
1950	223	—	223	25	248
1951	257	—	257	40	297
1952	252	—	252	31	283
1953	262		262	28	290

Year					
1955	272	▪	2,2	2⌐	⌐⌐⌐
1956	273	78	351	41	392
1957	271	93	364	59	423
1958	272	80	352	51	403
1959	275	79	354	31	385
1960	275	80	355	33	388
1961	270	72	342	134	476
1962	253	56	309	123	432
1963	249	69	318	111	429
1964	236	70	306	125	431
1965	235	59	294	154	448
1966	219	37	256	219	475
1967	209	42	251	246	497
1968	203	47	250	206	456
1969	217	97	314	232	546
1970	250	95	345	287	632
1971	547	8	555	17	572
1972	522	28	550	34	584
1973	483	13	496	24	520
1974	506	—	506	47	553
1975	533	—	533	27	560
1976	474	—	474	25	499

*Detailed employees as of June 30 each year.
SOURCE: Compiled from White House information and the OMB Records Office.

as to how much of this is necessary, and few who could describe the process by which the chief clerk's office and the Executive Office make sure that the papers are correctly drawn. Much of such paperwork is, of course, routine material and scarcely relevant to important issues of public policy. But disregard of such routine operations is suggestive of how little research has been accumulated that could be of practical help to new White House participants. What is most needed in current Presidential research is not history for its own sake but studies that contribute to our understanding of how central government performs and how it might perform better.

The problem of central government machinery is a serious one. If, as Presidential scholars assert, the White House has increasingly drawn more of the important policy-making activities into itself, then the Presidency has also become more vulnerable to a lack of institutional memory as White House occupants come and go. Participants may well become less and less able to answer important questions such as: What kind of problem is this? Who needs to be brought in it? How was it, or a similar problem, approached in previous administrations? Unfortunately, only since the controversies over the Nixon papers have there been serious efforts to limit the private disposition of papers used by leading figures while in public office and thus increase access to them by successors and scholars[7].

7. These questions have been studied by the Commission on Public Documents in Washington, D.C., Robert Brookhart, Executive Director. The ex-

Academic research on the Presidency has added very little to the already weak capacity of the White House to draw lessons from the experience of previous administrations. After more than two decades of working in the Executive Office on problems of government organization and reorganization, for example, one of the nation's leading experts in this area reported:

We've had almost no systematic analysis to determine what in fact reorganization achieves. This was one of my great frustrations when I was responsible for the President's reorganization program. We never had the time or staff to analyze the results of reorganization.[8]

What was said about government reorganization can be said for almost any problem confronting the Presidency. Government offices and former White House officials have little opportunity to conduct research on "what happened the last time." And once out of office they have little incentive to pursue a critical analysis of their own work, certainly not in such a way that might be of use to successors.

Academics rarely fill this gap. The absence of problem-

tent to which FDR relied on experienced White House clerks in organizing his West Wing office is usually forgotten. In the case of officials such as Ira Smith or Robert Lincoln O'Brien, the experience went back to the McKinley and Cleveland administrations. At the news conference announcing creation of the new Executive Office of the President, newsmen laughed at the notion of finding Presidential aides with "a passion for anonymity," and Roosevelt pointed to the longtime Chief Clerk in the White House, Rudolph Foster, as a real-life example of what he had in mind. (Louis Brownlow, *The President and the Presidency* (1949), p. 61.) Foster's successor, William Hopkins, served from FDR's Presidency until midway into the Nixon administration.

8. Harold Seidman, "Executive Reorganization," *Public Administration Review* (1974), p. 489.

oriented research on the Presidency becomes painfully apparent during every transition period between administrations. An incoming administration that tries to reach out beyond the briefing books hurriedly prepared by the bureaucracy is likely to find that very little scholarship is available to help it solve some of the most basic questions in organizing the Presidency: How has the appointment process for political executives actually worked and how can it be improved?[9] Why have efforts at management rarely succeeded?[10] What are the deficiencies in the executive budgeting process and what, in the light of past experience, will improve chances for successful budget reform? How can a President intervene in the details he most cares about without adding to White House problems by bureaucratizing presidential staff? What do Presidents know and when do they know it? How can they get early warning of new problems and keep track of how well their decisions towards solving old problems are being implemented?

The Carter campaign organization made an extensive effort to draw on leading experts to prepare reports and option papers on the Presidency (as well as many other fields). While these memoranda remain private, it is

9. The first extended analysis of this question appeared only in the last year: Calvin Mackenzie, *The Appointment Process: The Selection and Confirmation of Federal Political Executives* (1975).

10. Among several recent works that make an effort in this direction are William Medina, "Factors Which Condition the Responses of Departments and Agencies to Centrally Mandated Management Improvement Approaches," American University, 1976; and Richard Rose, *Managing Presidential Objectives* (1976).

40

certain that very few of them were based upon any detailed comparative analysis of what had happened in government operations during the previous decade or so. Indeed, advice on White House organization is as likely as not to repeat the familiar theme that a President must maintain complete flexibility in staff arrangements—thus implicitly denying that different administrations have anything in common with regard to work flow, problems, and consequences of choices. Since solid research is lacking, truisms abound: A small White House staff might be inadequate to cope with the Presidential workload but a large staff could get the President in trouble; A hierarchical organization would prevent confusion in responsibilities, but it would reduce redundancy in the information a President needs for cross-checking his sources. Insofar as such truisms have empirical backing, it is frequently based on selective memory rather than on a dispassionate description or analysis of conditions and problems common to different administrations. As one Presidential scholar put it, "The advice of the 60s is being repeated for 1976 and it's going to be no better or worse than it was in 1960, even though much more evidence has intervened since then."

Organization of economic advice in the Presidency is another good example of the current lack of operationally relevant research, a state of affairs lamented by many economists with experience in Washington.[11]

11. Herbert Stein, *Economic Planning and the Improvement of Economic Policy* (1975); Arthur Okun, "The Formulation of National Economic Pol-

Some experts are presently urging the creation of a new micro economic capability in the Executive Office to organize Presidential advice on wages and prices by industrial sector, but much of the planning for this capability by economists, businessmen, and others is going forward with little knowledge of similar attempts that have periodically been made in the past. A recent study using primary source material in the Presidential libraries documents how our postwar experience has repeated previous trials and errors (particularly the latter) and suggests a number of lessons that should be drawn from this documentation. As one author observed:

A striking feature of the story recorded here is the short institutional memory of the economic advisory arms of government. Repeatedly, circumstances and policy measures...were discussed as if they had never occurred or been proposed before. The phenomenon is largely the result of the presidential form of government wherein each new chief executive brings in his own advisers and sweeps out the old. Nevertheless the observer cannot help wondering if more provision for the accumulation of wisdom and experience might not be valuable. To an important degree this function was performed in an informal way by a dozen or so prominent persons who

---

icy," *Perspective in Defense Management* (1968); "Comments of Paul McCracken," Princeton Conference on Presidential Advisors, November 1975. An excellent case can be made for economists to "help reverse the trend to disinvest in history by shifting some resources away from the study of the theory of economic policy and toward the study of how policies were made and executed...." See James L. Cochrane, "The U.S. Presidential Libraries and the History of Political Economy," *History of Political Economy,* Vol. 8, No. 3, Fall 1976.

appeared to deal with wage-price problems in several administrations....But should an important social system have to depend on such accidents of fate?[12]

There is, of course, no guarantee that even if there were a supply of operationally relevant research on the Presidency, policy-makers would be interested in it. But it is reasonable to think there will be a growing demand for such research as more questions are raised about government capabilities to do at least some things well and as policy-makers become more hard-pressed to show that they can make the executive branch work competently. If nothing else, such research could present a more balanced and empirically based picture of the Presidency than one receives from the current preponderance of writing about the personal dramas surrounding a particular President and his crisis decisions. Breaking out of the existing pattern will require more comparative analysis across administrations, not in order to rate Presidents, but to identify common problems, processes, and lessons. Such comparative studies (discouraged by among other things the geographical dispersion of Presidential libraries) are in extraordinarily short supply.[13]

12. Craufurd D. Goodwin, *Exhortation and Controls* (1975), p. 7.

13. There are, of course, many passing references to different Presidents in the literature, but only a few works (such as Neustadt and Hess) pursue such comparisons. The previously cited Greenstein bibliography lists the following among the prominent comparative studies: Arthur Krock, *Memoirs: Intimate Recollections of Twelve American Presidents* (1970); E. Lincoln, *Kennedy and Johnson* (1968); W.A. Wilson, *Some Presidents: Wilson to Nixon* (1972); C.V. Woodward(ed.), *Responses of the Presidents to Charges of Misconduct* (1974).

3. *The Preponderance of Political Scientists.* Citations in the first section of this report leave little doubt that a great deal of the academic work on the Presidency has been done by political scientists. In a few cases (Irving James, Alexander George, James David Barber) scholars with a professional interest in psychology have made noteworthy attempts to broaden Presidential research perspective but apart from these and many historical works, it is difficult to find literature on the modern Presidency that is not written by political scientists.

Obviously political scientists will always play an important part in Presidential research. But there is reason to question whether political scientists, acting without collaboration with other social scientists, can give us a sufficiently broad understanding of the Presidency. The professional skills of historians, for example, are often necessary for effective use of primary material in Presidential archives even if the history in question is more recent than that usually falling under historians' jurisdiction. In addition, problem-oriented research on the Presidency often requires the contribution of experts in a particular area of substantive policy, as, for example, economists' use of Presidential papers in assessing the postwar lessons of United States wage-price policy (Goodwin, *Exhortations and Controls,* 1975). Even for understanding the "public administration" of the Presidency (the organization, staff responsibilities, work flow, advice, and information systems in the White House), a traditional public administration approach may be insufficient. Political scientists' frequent references to court politics, staff feuds, the President's chieftainship, and so on all suggest a need for sensitivity to the social organization of the Presidency and executive politics. Research progress in this direction may well depend less on political scientists and more on social anthropologists, sociologists, and other such professionals who are interested in the culture and tribal politics of their own government.[14]

14. Some promising beginnings along these lines are E.G. Bailey, *Stratagems and Spoils* (1969); Jeremy Boissevain, *Friends of Friends* (1974); M. Komarovsky, *Sociology and Public Policy: The Case of the Presidential Commissions* (1975).

RESOURCES:
TOWARD MORE PRODUCTIVE RESEARCH

In terms of basic material with which to pursue more adequate studies of the Presidency, data resources are now probably greater than at any time in the past. While the first Presidential Library is slightly over thirty years old, it is only since the mid-1950s that there has been any general provision for preserving Presidential papers and for opening them to scholarly research. Prior to the Presidential Library Act of 1955 (45 U.S.C. 2101) such papers were dispersed, often retained by heirs, sometimes burned or otherwise destroyed, and only long after an administration had passed into history purchased by the government and made available to the public.[1] Since the early 1950s, almost all of FDR's papers have been opened; Herbert Hoover's material has been collected and trans-

1. A brief history of the disposition of every President's papers is given in *Examination of President Nixon's Tax Returns for 1969-1972*, House Report No. 966, 93 Cong. I sess. (1974), App. pp. A76-A83. Useful information on Presidential libraries is contained in Richard S. Kirkendahl, "A Second Look at Presidential Libraries," *American Archivist* (1966); C.E. Vose, "Presidential Papers as a Political Science Concern," *P.S.* (1975); J.L. Cole, "Presidential Libraries," *Journal of Librianship* (1974); H.G. Jones, "Presidential Libraries: Is There a Case for a National Presidential Library?" *American Archivist* (1975).

ferred to a central facility, and, during the 1960s, the doors of new Presidential libraries for Truman, Eisenhower, Kennedy, and Johnson were opened to researchers.

In all of these libraries the research material is of four general types (in addition to audio-visual information and memorabilia): 1) original or photocopied documents; 2) oral histories; 3) collections of private papers from persons associated with a particular President; and 4) published work relevant to that particular Presidential term. There is a consensus, especially among archival staffs working in the newer libraries, that there has been little serious use of this material to gain an understanding of how the Presidency works.[2] Here are representative comments from archivists in the Kennedy and Johnson libraries:

People who come here looking for intimate or personal details aren't going to find them in open material. But for getting an idea of the process and official duties, for getting a real understanding of the office, it's almost all here. In that respect, this place hasn't been touched yet.

A second archivist, specializing in mandatory review and declassification of defense and foreign policy papers, reported:

Most of the Vietnam material is now being declassified. What you generally get are not the bombshells but a vast amount of

2. The Truman Library appears to have gone furthest in trying to create a general research resource on the Presidency. See Richard Kirkendahl, *The Truman Period as a Research Field* (1967) and *The Truman Period as a Research Field. A Reappraisal* (1974).

information on day-to-day operations, telegraph exchanges, and things like that. For serious scholars it is a fantastic resource…. Take the National Security files: There you can see all the weekend papers and cover memos that were going to the President from his special assistant. It shows you what the President was being told every week on the leading issues of the day. People who have used this have just taken a bit here and there and incorporated it into their study of a particular issue or case. But looked at as a whole it's a terrific source of documentation on how the White House was actually working. As far as I can tell, no one is studying how the Presidency as such operates.

There are, of course, important limitations to the Presidential library as a research resource. A number of former officials in government have retained the papers they used while in public office; hence Presidential libraries may not give a fully rounded picture. Even though requests have been made for the review and declassification of virtually all the material in these libraries, a considerable number of these requests have not been heeded. Lack of library manpower may cause research delays even after efforts to open closed material have been successful[3] Probably the most important limitation is the very massiveness of the libraries' collections, which can

3. For example, under Presidential Order (E.O. 11652) for mandatory review of classified materials, some 4,000 pages a year have been declassified during the last two years at the Kennedy Library, but its holdings of classified documents runs up to 1 million pages. The point is that researchers who cannot afford to wait need a fairly clear idea of the specific material they want for special review. The various registers and finding guides in each library are a major asset, and the archivists in Presidential libraries are frequently most helpful in making appeals to open closed material.

easily overpower an inexperienced researcher, especially one with a poorly defined project. Clearly, however, none of these problems is particularly substantial when one considers the need for more reliable basic research on the Presidency and the opportunities these libraries offer to meet this need.

Research opportunities have also been recently broadened by the Freedom of Information Act. Under this law, the previous normal waiting period—in some cases fifteen years or more—for access to executive branch documents has been reduced considerably. While there are a large number of exceptions (among which are top executives' communications) and roadblocks to implementation, a well-defined research project should be able to use this legal instrument to gain information on everyday Presidential operations, particularly as these affect actions in the wider bureaucracy. However, it seems that so far the Freedom of Information Act has been little used by academic researchers. Its use has been largely confined to private law firms and interest groups with a specific interest in a particular agency's activities.

Unlike data resources, financial resources for research on the Presidency are quite limited. Three of the Presidential libraries (Truman, Johnson and Roosevelt) offer small grants of up to $1,000 for scholars wishing to make use of their particular library. The National Science Foundation and several other government agencies have supported studies on the Presidency but appear reluctant to sponsor politically sensitive research on White House operations or critical analysis of performance by former administrations. Established writers on the Presidency have periodically gained support from a number of different foundations (such as Carnegie, the Twentieth Century Fund, Russell Sage) or from special lecture series. The Center for the Study of the Presidency does not function as a significant funding source for original research on the Presidency and the American Political Science Association has no research apparatus equivalent to its Committee for the Study of Congress. A number of smaller foundations offer small grants or loans, but generally these are far below the amount needed to support original research over the course of a year or more. The Brookings Institution and more recently the American Enterprise Institute have provided what is perhaps the only concentrated source of private funding for study of government institutions in Washington.

In sum, basic research on the Presidency suffers from a lack of sustained, well-focused support. The geographical dispersion of Presidential libraries is itself a deterrent to research leading to generalizations about the Presidency, as opposed to research on individual Presidents. Similarly, existing funding sources do not promote the time-consuming, basic research necessary for comparative analysis of Presidencies and improvement of central government performance.

CONCLUSION

If past experience is any guide, many approaches to studying the Presidency will prosper without any outside encouragement. Memoirs and retrospective accounts will continue to be written by former White House participants. These, in turn, will produce more material for secondary analysis by academic writers on the Presidency. A steady flow of popular interpretations of "the man" will offer fascinating personal information (and undoubtedly sell well). Political scientists will go on writing or editing works to assess the latest ups and downs of Presidential power. Major crises will continue to be described in case studies of particularly dramatic decisions.

The justification for any additional funding in this already immense field seems clear: Such support could provide incentives for types of Presidential studies that otherwise will continue to be neglected. Proper funding could encourage research to focus less on the headline events and personalities of a given administration and more on the nonglamorous, everyday operation of the Presidency. Such research should have four characteristics. It should:

1. concentrate on processes and behavior in the White House and the Executive Office of the President;

2. describe, explain, and evaluate experiences in more than one administration;

3. make use of primary materials and documentation to be found in Presidential libraries and elsewhere;

4. concentrate on recurring problems that are likely to be relevant for future administrations.

No restriction on subject matter or disciplinary approach is implied in these guidelines, although researchers should bear in mind the classification restraints and delays involved in opening current materials in the fields of national security and foreign policy. The following is a representative, though not exhaustive, list of the kinds of topics that could highlight common institutional problems and draw lessons across administrations:

—how Presidents spend their time and to what effect

—politics and coordination of economic policy-making

—evolution of staff performance in the Executive Office of the President

—developing problems of the executive budget process

—Presidential information: what Presidents know and how they know it

—the role and control of partisan politics in White House operations

—Presidential management strategies for dealing with the bureaucracy, Congress, and interest groups.

More research of the kind suggested here will not necessarily provide specific answers to the problems facing a particular President, but it could help improve the chances that any problem will be confronted with a better background of information and more seasoned judgment. For the public at large such research might help counteract some of the mystery and majestic pretensions that naturally surround the office. In fact, maintaining an empirical, sensible perspective on the Presidency as an ongoing institution may be the chief and most enduring contribution that Presidential scholars can make. For as Augustus Woodward noted about the Chief Executive almost 170 years ago, "The man, constantly surrounded by his personal friends; the companion only of his flatterers and dependents; loses, by degrees, a just sense of himself."

37-301